MANUAL FOR MUSHROOMS

How to Grow Mushrooms
in Six Easy Steps

IAN MCNEELY

Table of Contents

CHAPTER ONE

The raising of mushrooms

How to Grow Mushrooms in Six Easy Steps

Each step in mushroom farming can be broken down into six different categories, but these categories are still useful because they show what is required to set up a production system in the first place.

Initiation

Composting is the first step.

In the second stage,

Composting is another option.

3. Reproduction

The Enclosure

The fifth step is pinning.

Aspect Ratio

When describing these steps, the author emphasizes the most important aspects of each step. Mushrooms require nutrients from compost to grow. Wheat straw-bedded horse manure is the most common and least expensive type of mushroom compost. The most common ingredients in synthetic compost are hay and crushed corncobs, but the term can also refer to any mushroom compost that does not contain horse manure as its primary ingredient. Nitrogen supplements and gypsum, a conditioning agent, are required for both types of compost.

Phase I and Phase II composting are the two stages of the composting process. We'll start with Phase I composting before moving on to mushroom cultivation.

Phase one:

Making Compost from Mushrooms

Composting in an enclosed structure or a structure with a

roof over it is more common than not, but it is not unheard of. Composting necessitates the use of a concrete slab known as a wharf. Additional equipment is required, including a composter that turns the ingredients and a tractor-loader that moves the ingredients into place. Pitchforks were used in the past to turn piles manually, which is still an option, but it is labor- and physically-intensive.

Mixing and wetting the ingredients as they are stacked in a rectangular pile with tight sides and a loose center is the first step in Phase I composting. Compost turners are commonly used to process the bulk ingredients. Horse manure and synthetic compost are sprayed with water as they move through the turner. The turner distributes nitrogen supplements and gypsum over the bulk ingredients and thoroughly mixes them. Upon moistening and forming the pile, aerobic fermentation (composting) begins as a result of microorganism growth and reproduction in the bulk ingredients. During this process, ammonia and carbon dioxide are released. Activators for compost other than those mentioned are not required, despite the emphasis in some organic farming books.

Mushroom compost is created when microorganisms, heat, and chemical reactions that release heat change the chemical nature of the raw ingredients. When these things happen, the mushroom gets what it needs to grow, and other fungi or bacteria are left out. You can't go through the process without the right amount of moisture, oxygenation, nitrogen, and carbs. This is why the compost pile is aerated as it passes through the turner and water and supplements are added on a regular basis.

The addition of gypsum reduces the greasiness of compost. There are some chemicals that tend to clump together when they come into contact with gypsum, and these chemicals stick together rather than filling the gaps (holes) between straws. Air is essential to the composting process because of this phenomenon, and it can more easily permeate the pile.

The absence of air results in an anaerobic environment in which harmful chemical compounds are formed, reducing the selectivity of mushroom compost for mushroom growth. Composting begins with the addition of 40 lbs. of gypsum per ton of dry ingredients.

Brewer's grain, seed meals of soybeans, peanuts, or cotton, and chicken manure are among the most commonly used nitrogen supplements today. For horse manure and synthetic, the goal is to raise the nitrogen content from 1.5% to 1.7%,

CHAPTER TWO

both in terms of dry weight. Microflora in synthetic compost must be supplied with ammonium nitrate or urea as soon as possible to ensure that they can grow and reproduce effectively.

Corn cobs can be difficult to come by, or they can be purchased at a price that is considered excessive. Cottonseed hulls, neutralized grape pomace and cocoa bean hulls can be substitutes for or complements to the corn cob. The watering and turning intervals for compost piles containing any one of these materials are unique.

5-6 feet wide by 5-6 feet high by as long as necessary is a good starting point for a compost pile. Some turners have a "ricker," which eliminates the need for a box when forming the pile (rick). During Phase I composting, the sides of the pile should be firm and dense, but the center must remain open. During composting, the straw or hay softens, making it easier for compactions to form. Anaerobic conditions can develop in a pile if the materials are compacted too much.

You should turn and water the pile about once every two days unless it is extremely hot (145° to 170°F). As a result of turning the pile, you can water, aerate and mix the ingredients, as well as move straw or hay from an area that is cooler to a more warm area. When the ricks are turned, supplements can also be added, but they should be added at the beginning of the composting process. How many times and how long it takes for the compost to heat to temperatures above 145°F are determined by the quality of the starting material and the time it takes for the compost to reach that temperature.

Over- or under-watering can limit bacterial and fungal growth by obstructing oxygen flow through the pores. When the pile is first formed and the first turn occurs, water is typically added up to the point of leaching, and then either none or only a small amount is added for the duration of the composting process. Compost can be watered liberally on the final turning before Phase II composting, so that when the compost is squeezed tightly, water drips out of it. Water, nutritive value, microbial activity, and temperature are all linked in a chain, and when one link breaks, the entire chain stops working. The Law of Limiting Factors has been coined by biologists to describe this phenomenon.

In the first phase of the composting process, the amount of time varies from 7 to 14 days, depending on the starting material and the characteristics of the compost at each turning. Composting emits a strong ammonia odor, which is often accompanied by a sweet, moldy aroma. Ammonia-induced chemical changes produce a food that is primarily consumed by mushrooms when compost temperatures reach 155°F or higher. Because of the chemical changes, heat builds up and compost temperatures rise. During the second and third turnings, compost temperatures can rise to 170° to 180°F if a desirable level of biological and chemical activity is taking place. As of the end of Phase I, the compost should look like chocolate; it should have soft, pliable straws; and it should have an ammonia-like smell. Phase I composting is complete when the specified levels of moisture, temperature, color, and odor are achieved.

This is the second phase

Phase II composting serves two primary purposes. If the

compost contains any insects, nematodes, pathogenic fungi, or other pests, they must be killed through the process of pasteurization. To begin with, the ammonia that accumulated during the initial composting process must be removed. It is necessary to remove ammonia at the end of Phase II if the concentration is greater than 0.07 percent because it is lethal to mushroom spawn growth. Ammonia can be smelled at concentrations greater than 0.10 percent.

Depending on the production system, Phase II can take place in one of three locations. Compost is packed into wooden trays, stacked six to eight high, and moved into an environmentally controlled Phase II room as part of the zoned system of growing. In the following stages, the trays are moved to different rooms, each of which is designed to provide the ideal conditions for the growth of mushrooms. Compost is placed directly in the beds in the room used for all stages of crop culture using a bed or shelf system. Compost is placed in a cement-block bin with a perforated floor and no cover over it in the bulk system, which is a room designed specifically for Phase II composting.

Compost should be compacted to the same depth and density whether it is placed in a bed, tray, or in bulk. Compost density must allow for gas exchange because outside air will replace ammonia and carbon dioxide.

During the second phase of composting, air is used to keep the compost at a temperature where de-ammonifying organisms can thrive and reproduce in a controlled, temperature-dependent manner. There must be readily available carbohydrates and nitrogen for these thermophilic (heat-loving) organisms to grow. Some nitrogen must be available as ammonia.

It is difficult to define optimal Phase II management, and commercial growers tend to use one of the two general systems in use today: high- or low-temperature.

CHAPTER THREE

During the initial pasteurization period, the compost and the air temperature are raised to at least 145°F for at least six hours. A combination of natural microorganism growth heat and steam injection into the room where the compost has been placed can accomplish this. Compost that has been pasteurized is immediately flushed with fresh air to cool it down to 140°F. When all the ammonia has been dispersed, the compost is allowed to cool at a rate of about 2° to 3°F per day. In order to complete this

Phase II system, allow 10-14 days of your time.

The compost in the low temperature Phase II system is heated to a range of 125° to 130°F using steam or the heat released by microbial growth before the air temperature is lowered again. Once the ammonia has dissipated, the compost temperature can be lowered by 2°F per day for 4 to 5 days following pasteurization.

When trying to figure out the best course of action, keep in mind what the goals of Phase II are. Its primary function is to remove ammonia. Temperatures between 125 and 130 degrees Fahrenheit are ideal for the growth of de-ammonifying microorganisms, which thrive in this range. Phase II also has the goal of pasteurizing the compost to kill any pests that may be present.

Before spawning (planting) can begin, the compost temperature must be lowered to approximately 75° to 80°F. Compost should have a nitrogen content of 2% to 4% and a moisture content of 68% to

72%. For a successful mushroom harvest, a bed or tray should have 5 to 7 lbs. of dry compost per square foot by the time Phase II is complete. Compost and compost temperatures must be kept uniform during the Phase II process in order to ensure a homogenous final product.

3. Reproduction

If you want mushrooms to grow in your mushroom compost, you'll need to inoculate it with mushroom spawn. The mushroom, like the tomato, is a fruit of a plant, just like the tomato. The seeds found in the tomato can be used to start a new crop the following year. As tiny as the spores that form inside a mushroom cap may be, they can't be handled like seeds. Mushrooms grow from mycelium, which is a type of cell that resembles a fungus's stems and roots. Mycelium is the white thread-like plant found on decaying wood or moldy bread. Vegetative propagation of mycelium is possible, just as with daffodil bulbs and the subsequent production of more daffodil plants. To ensure that the mycelium of mushrooms is not mixed with the mycelium of other fungi, specialized facilities are needed to propagate mycelium. Commercial mushroom growers buy spawn from one of about a dozen spawn companies. Mycelium propagated vegetatively is known as spawn.

Sterilization begins with sterilization of water and chalk in combination with rye grain; other small grains can be used in place of the rye in the spawning process. Block or brick spawn, or manure spawn, was used as a growth medium for spawn until about 1940, and this was known as sterilized horse manure formed into blocks. Such spawn is rare today. The grain and mycelium are shaken three times at 4-day intervals over a 14-day period of active mycelial growth after the grain has been sterilized. Once the mycelium has taken hold of the grain, the product is known as spawn. Spawn can be kept refrigerated for a few months, so farmers order spawn in advance.

Mushroom growers in the United States can select from four main cultivars: The four most common varieties are: smooth white, off-white, cream, and brown. Smooth white has a cap that is smooth, with a cap and stalk that are all white. Cream white has a cap that is smooth, with a stalk that is white, and a cap that is white to cream. There are up to eight smooth white strains to choose from within each of the four major groups. Mushroom isolates differ in flavor, texture, and cultivation requirements, but they are all mushrooms in every way. Soups and sauces typically call for white or off-white cultivars, but fresh mushrooms of any color can be enjoyed.

The spawn is strewn across the compost and thoroughly mixed in. For years, this was done by hand, using a small rake-like tool to spread the spawn across the compost's surface and ruffle it in. However, in recent years, a special spawning machine has been used to mix compost and spawn with tines or small finger-like devices for the bed system. As the compost moves on a conveyor belt or falls from a conveyor into a tray, the spawn is mixed into the compost. There should be at least one quart of spawn per 10 square feet of bed surface; this is considered ideal. In some cases, the rate is calculated by comparing the weight of the spawn to the weight of the compost; a spawning rate of 2% is ideal.

The temperature of the compost is kept at 75°F, and the relative humidity is kept high, to prevent the compost surface or the spawn from drying. The spawn will grow in these conditions, resulting in a web of mycelium that weaves throughout the compost. One biological entity is formed when the mycelium from different grains of compost fuse together into a single spawned bed of mycelium. After fusion, the spawn appears as a white to blue-white mass in the compost. Because of the heat generated by the spawn, if the compost temperature rises above 80° to 85°F (depending on the cultivar), the mycelium may be destroyed, preventing the compost from producing its maximum crop yield or quality mushrooms. Spawn growth slows and the harvesting window grows longer at temperatures below 74 degrees Fahrenheit.

Spawning rate, distribution, moisture, and temperature all play a role in how long it takes for spawn to colonize a given area of a compost pile. Typically, a full spawn run takes anywhere from 14 to 21 days. The compost will be ready for the next stage of production once it has been fully grown with spawn.

CHAPTER FOUR

Top-dressing is applied to the spawn-run compost on which mushrooms grow. Using clay-loam field soil, peat moss with ground limestone, or reclaimed weathered, spent compost as a casing is an option for growing plants. A water reservoir and a place for rhizomorphs to grow, casing does not require nutrients. Rhizomorphs, which look like long, thick strings, are formed when mycelium of a very fine texture combines into a single substance. There are no mushrooms without rhizomorphs, which produce mushroom initials, primordia, or pins. To ensure that it is free of insects and pathogens, the container should be pasteurized. In addition, the casing must be distributed evenly across the compost's surface in order to maintain uniform depth. Mushrooms will grow at the same rate because of this uniformity in how spawn moves through the casing. The ability of the casing to retain moisture is critical for the growth of a firm mushroom.

For up to five days after casing, the compost temperature must be kept at or near 75°F, and the relative humidity must be high in order to properly manage the crop. When small mushroom initials (pins) begin to form, the compost temperature should be lowered by 2 degrees Fahrenheit each day. Water must be applied intermittently for the duration of the time following casing in order to raise the moisture level to field capacity prior to the formation of mushroom pins. Expert growers can tell the difference between novices and experts by knowing when, how, and how much water to apply to casing.

The fifth step is pinning.

It is only after the rhizomorphs have formed in the casing that mushrooms develop their initials. Rhizomorphic outgrowths bear the initials, which are minuscule but visible. The structure becomes a pin after the initial quadruple in size.. During the button stage, pins continue to grow in size until they reach the size of a mushroom. After 18 to 21 days of casing, edible mushrooms begin to appear. If fresh air is brought in, the carbon dioxide content of the room air drops to 0.08 percent or less, depending on the cultivar. The carbon dioxide concentration in the ambient air is approximately 0.04 percent.

Fresh air introduction must be timed carefully, and this is something that can only be learned through trial and error. Watering should be stopped when pin initials begin to form, and ventilating should be minimized until the mycelium can be seen poking through the surface of the casing. By lowering the carbon dioxide level too early, the mycelium stops growing through the casing and mushroom initials form below the surface of the casing.. Dirty mushrooms grow through the casing as they mature, so harvesting them is a messy process. As a result of insufficient moisture, mushrooms may grow beneath your casing. Pinning is an important step in the production process because it has an impact on both the yield and quality of a crop.

Aspect Ratio

There are three distinct harvest periods during a cropping cycle: a flush, a break, and a bloom. Harvesting can continue for as long as the mushrooms continue to mature in this rhythmic cycle. Farmers typically pick for 35 to 42 days, but some pick for 60 days or more, and some even continue picking for 150 days or more.

For best results, keep the air temperature at 57° to 62°F during cropping. Disease pathogens and insect pests can both live longer lives in this temperature range because it favors mushroom growth. There may seem to be an oddity in the fact that mushrooms are vulnerable to pests, but there is no crop that does not face competition from other organisms. Mushroom pests can cause complete crop failures, and the level of pest infestation often determines how long to harvest a crop. However, these organisms can be controlled using cultural practices and pesticides. It is preferable to keep these organisms out of the growing rooms altogether.

Growing rooms should have high enough relative humidity to prevent casing from drying out but not so high that developing mushrooms' caps become clammy or sticky. So that the mushrooms do not suffer from water stress, water is applied to the casing on a regular basis in commercial settings, usually two to three times per week. In some cases, more or less gallons of water may be used per watering, depending on factors such as how dry the casing is, the cultivar, and the stage in development of the mushrooms. For the most part, novice growers use too much water, which causes the casing's surface to seal and lose its texture. The exchange of gases necessary for the formation of mushroom pins is prevented by a sealed casing. After harvesting the first break, one can estimate how much water to add by considering that 90% of the mushroom is water and a gallon of water weighs 8.3 lbs. It is necessary to replenish the casing's water supply after harvesting 100 pounds of mushrooms, which removes 90 pounds of water (11 gallons).

During the harvest period, harvesters use outside air to regulate the temperature of both the air and the compost. Carbon dioxide from the growing mycelium is also displaced by the outside air. Fresh air is needed more during the first two breaks because of the increased growth of mycelial organisms, which produces carbon dioxide. The amount of fresh air also depends on the growing mushrooms, the surface area of the producing surface, the amount of compost in the growing room, and the condition or composition of the fresh air that is being introduced into the space. If the compost is 8 inches deep, the volume of air required is 0.3ft/hr and 50% to 100% of this volume must be outside air. While mushrooms are growing, there is a common question about whether or not they need light. Only green plants, such as mushrooms, require light for photosynthesis in order to grow.

CHAPTER FIVE

To make harvesting and crop practices easier, growing rooms can be illuminated. However, workers and mushroom farmers are more commonly provided with miner's lamps than an entire room is lit.

Mushroom cultivation requires ventilation, as well as control over humidity and temperature. A cold mist, live steam, or simply wetting the walls and floors can add moisture to the air. To remove moisture from a growing room, you can do one of three things: 1) bring in more outside air; 2) bring in dry air; or 3) bring in the same amount of outside air and heat it to a higher temperature, which lowers the relative humidity because warmer air holds more moisture. Mushroom growing rooms use the same principles of temperature control as your own home. Water circulated through wall-mounted pipes can generate heat. Forcing hot air through a ventilation duct is a common practice in newly constructed mushroom farms. Some mushroom farms are located in limestone caves, where the rock acts as both a heating and cooling surface depending on the season. Not all caves are suitable for mushroom growing, and abandoned coal mines have too many inherent issues to be considered viable locations for a mushroom farm. To grow mushrooms in limestone caves, extensive renovation and improvement is required. Only the growing takes place in the cave, with composting taking place on a wharf above ground.

If the temperature, humidity, cultivar, and stage at which the mushrooms are harvested are all taken into consideration, the harvesting period can be anywhere from seven to ten days. When mature mushrooms are harvested, a growth inhibitor is removed, allowing the next flush of mushrooms to mature more quickly. A time when the veil isn't too thick is ideal for picking mushrooms. Open, flat mushrooms are more popular in England and Australia than closed, tight mushrooms are in North America. A mushroom's maturity is determined by the length of its veil, not by its size. As a result, mature mushrooms can be large or small, but farmers and consumers alike prefer medium- to large-sized mushrooms..

The methods used to pick and package produce can vary widely from farm to farm. Frozen mushrooms must be kept at 35° to 45°F for at least 24 hours after harvesting. Mushrooms need to be allowed to "breathe" after harvest in order to extend their shelf life, so nonwaxed paper bags are preferred to plastic bags for storage.

Immediately after harvesting the last batch of mushrooms, the growing room should be sealed off and steam-pasteurized. If there are pests lurking around in the growing room, this final pasteurization is designed to kill them and prevent them from spreading to the next crop.

Conclusion

It takes about 15 weeks to complete a full production cycle, starting with composting and ending with the final steaming off after harvesting is finished. In 1980, the national average for this work was 3.12 lbs. per square foot, with a range from 0 to 4 lbs. Temperature, humidity, pests, and other environmental factors all play a role in final yield. All things considered, experience and an intuitive understanding of the commercial mushroom's biological rhythms appear to be the most important factors for successful production. After the fundamentals of mushroom growing are understood, the production system for a crop can be selected.

THE END